OKLAHOMA

Helen Lepp Friesen

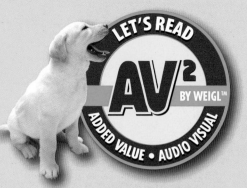

LET'S READ
AV²
BY WEIGL™
ADDED VALUE • AUDIO VISUAL

Go to **www.av2books.com,** and enter this book's unique code.

BOOK CODE

L1570

AV² by Weigl brings you media enhanced books that support active learning.

AV² provides enriched content that supplements and complements this book. Weigl's AV² books strive to create inspired learning and engage young minds in a total learning experience.

Your AV² Media Enhanced books come alive with...

Audio
Listen to sections of the book read aloud.

Video
Watch informative video clips.

Embedded Weblinks
Gain additional information for research.

Try This!
Complete activities and hands-on experiments.

Key Words
Study vocabulary, and complete a matching word activity.

Quizzes
Test your knowledge.

Slide Show
View images and captions, and prepare a presentation.

... and much, much more!

Published by AV² by Weigl
350 5th Avenue, 59th Floor
New York, NY 10118
Website: www.av2books.com   www.weigl.com

Library of Congress Cataloging-in-Publication Data
Friesen, Helen Lepp, 1961-
Oklahoma / Helen Lepp Friesen.
   p. cm. -- (Explore the U.S.A.)
Includes bibliographical references and index.
ISBN 978-1-61913-391-4 (hard cover : alk. paper)
1. Oklahoma--Juvenile literature. I. Title.
F694.3.F75 2013
976.6--dc23
                    2012015612

Printed in the United States of America in North Mankato, Minnesota
1 2 3 4 5 6 7 8 9 16 15 14 13 12

052012
WEP040512

Project Coordinator: Karen Durrie
Art Director: Terry Paulhus

Weigl acknowledges Getty Images as the primary image supplier for this title.

OKLAHOMA

Contents

3

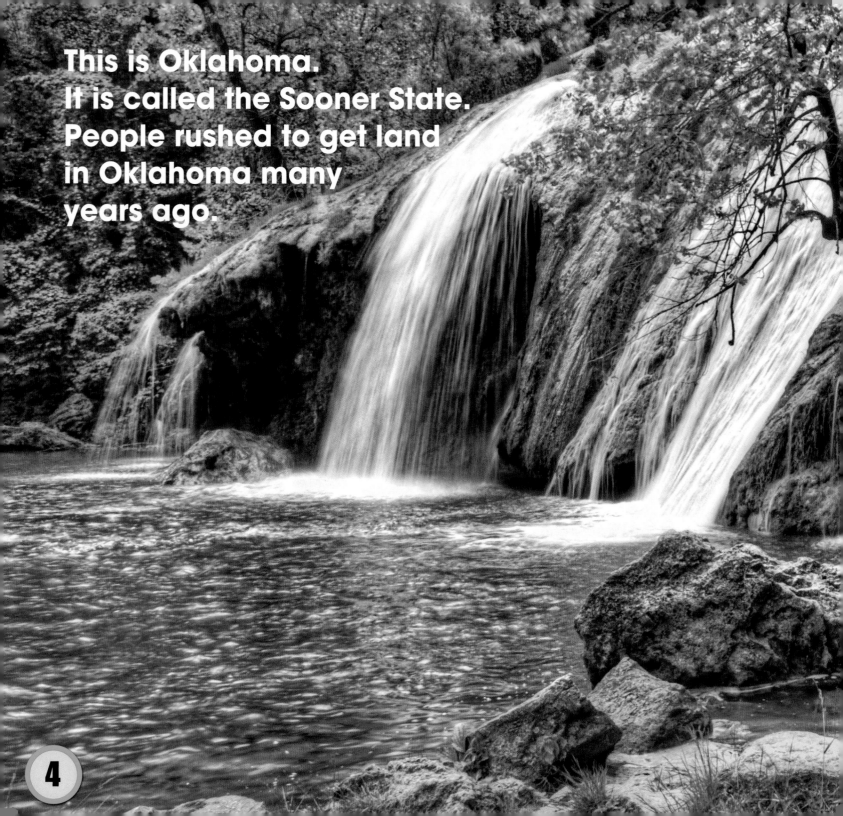

This is Oklahoma.
It is called the Sooner State.
People rushed to get land
in Oklahoma many
years ago.

4

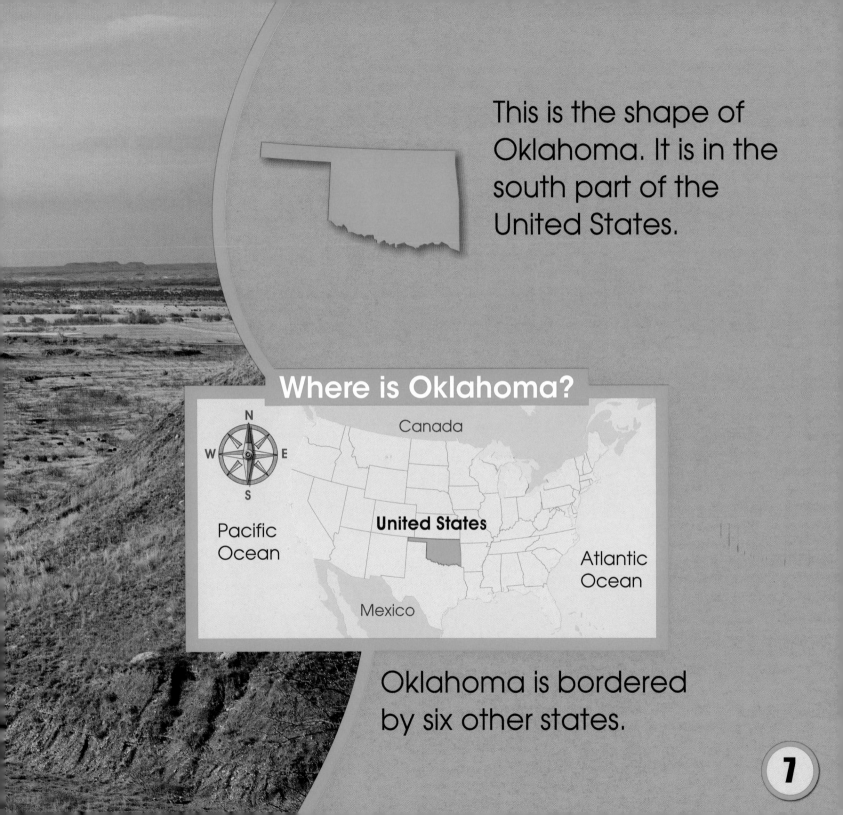

This is the shape of Oklahoma. It is in the south part of the United States.

Where is Oklahoma?

Canada

N
W   E
S

United States

Pacific Ocean

Atlantic Ocean

Mexico

Oklahoma is bordered by six other states.

Many settlers came to Oklahoma more than 100 years ago. This was called the Oklahoma Land Rush.

Settlers rode on wagons, trains, and horses to get land in Oklahoma.

The Oklahoma rose is the state flower. It makes a fruit called rose hip.

The Oklahoma state seal has a star with many pictures.

One picture has an American Indian and a settler shaking hands.

This is the state flag of
Oklahoma. It has an
American Indian shield
with seven eagle feathers.

The flag also has
an olive branch.

13

The state animal of Oklahoma is the American buffalo. American Indians hunted buffalo. They used it for food, clothes, and shelter.

A buffalo can weigh up to 2,000 pounds.

This is the biggest city in Oklahoma. It is called Oklahoma City. It is the state capital.

An oil well is next to the Oklahoma State capitol.

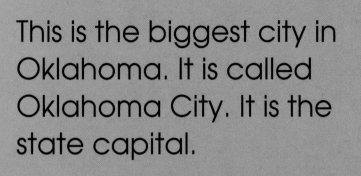

Wheat grows in Oklahoma. Wheat is the biggest crop in Oklahoma. It is used to make bread and cereal.

Oklahoma grows more than three million acres of wheat.

Oklahoma has a well known road called Route 66.

People stop along Route 66 to visit museums, parks, and gardens.

OKLAHOMA FACTS

These pages provide detailed information that expands on the interesting facts found in the book. These pages are intended to be used by adults as a learning support to help young readers round out their knowledge of each state in the *Explore the U.S.A.* series.

Pages 4–5

Congress designated Oklahoma as Indian Territory in 1828. After the Civil War, the government opened Oklahoma land to pioneers. During the Great Land Run in 1889, settlers lined up at the Oklahoma border. At the sound of a bugle, they rushed to get land. Those who started before the bugle sounded were nicknamed Sooners because they ran too soon.

Pages 6–7

On November 16, 1907, Oklahoma became the 46th state to join the United States. Oklahoma shares borders with Arkansas, Missouri, New Mexico, Colorado, Kansas, and Texas. The state's geography ranges from flat plains to mountains.

Pages 8–9

Oklahoma land was appropriated from American Indians to be opened to settlers in 1889. Settlers raced to claim tracts from 1.9 million acres (770,000 hectares) of land at noon on April 22, 1889. About 50,000 people rushed for 12,000 land tracts. Settlers kept arriving in Oklahoma until the land was gone. Several other land rushes took place at later times.

Pages 10–11

The Oklahoma rose was named the official state flower in 2004. American Indian tribes are symbolized on the state seal. They include the Chickasaw, Cherokee, Choctaw, Creek, and Seminole Nations. These nations still live in Oklahoma today. The 45 stars on the seal stand for the 45 states in existence when Oklahoma became a state.

KEY WORDS

Research has shown that as much as 65 percent of all written material published in English is made up of 300 words. These 300 words cannot be taught using pictures or learned by sounding them out. They must be recognized by sight. This book contains 47 common sight words to help young readers improve their reading fluency and comprehension. This book also teaches young readers several important content words, such as proper nouns. These words are paired with pictures to aid in learning and improve understanding.

Page	Sight Words First Appearance
4	get, in, is, it, land, many, people, state, the, this, to, years
7	by, of, other, part, where
8	and, came, more, on, than, was
11	a, American, an, hands, has, Indian, makes, one, pictures, with
12	also
15	animal, can, food, for, up, used
16	city, next, well
19	grows, three
21	along, stop

Page	Content Words First Appearance
4	Oklahoma, Sooner
7	shape, United States
8	horses, Oklahoma Land Rush, settlers, trains, wagons
11	flower, fruit, rose hip, seal, star
12	feathers, flag, olive branch, shield
15	buffalo, clothes, pounds, shelter
16	capital, capitol, Oklahoma City
19	acres, bread, cereal, crop, wheat
21	gardens, museums, parks, road, Route 66

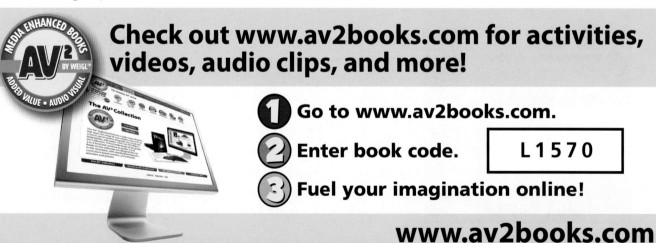